The Ethnosphere's Duality

Heath Brougher

Cyberwit.net

HIG 45 Kaushambi Kunj, Kalindipuram

Allahabad - 211011 (U.P.) India

http://www.cyberwit.net

Tel: +(91) 9415091004 +(91) (532) 2552257

E-mail: info@cyberwit.net

Printed at Repro India Limited.

INTRODUCTION

As the following quote by Nietzsche much more eloquently states, this book is not meant for everyone. It is meant, rather, for the people out there who are on a similar philosophical wavelength as myself. It is a very experimental book that probes the question "what causes something to exist?" and/or "what creates creation?" while examining the relationship between Consciousness and Existence. This is a book that I hope will open minds to begin questioning the very essence of life or at least start viewing certain aspects of it from a different angle. It is a book for ears that are "related" to mine.

"On the question of being understandable.— One does not only wish to be understood when one writes; one wishes just as surely *not* to be understood. It is not by any means necessarily an objection to a book when anybody finds it impossible to understand: perhaps that was part of the author's intention—he did not want to be understood by just "anybody." Every more noble spirit and taste selects its audience when it wishes to communicate itself; and choosing them, it at the same time erects barriers against "the others." All the more subtle laws of any style have their origin at this point: they at the same time keep away, create a distance, forbid "entrance," understanding, as said above—while they open the ears of those whose ears are related to ours."

-*Friedrich Nietzsche*

Contents

Lucky Number Never

You are part of the concoction
      you are a sliver of construction
never fully   realized or formed
      despite the Millennia of your attempted Rising
all that's left   are fragments
     strewn about the clouds
turned the color of summer storm
     this supposedly fleshed out thing was never fully fleshed out
because it was only ever a thought   a piece of the imagination
     of the various minds which   permeate the land

when one thinks deep enough   one realizes the conun-
drum:

         every Truth is also an unTruth.

The Verge

That which was to be determined
was disposed of precisely so it
would be void of any and all pose
[wholesome deprivation. nothing else]
unborn disposition, misinterpreted, unbred and unbegun,
disapprovals don't disavow the displacement
of things [*this*] placed in a Proximitous way
whether composed of thought or brick
it was disowned and purposefully predisposed of
before Conclusion could clutch its fragments strewn
into nothingness or wrap a head around the essence or anything at all so as
to have full augmentation and no argumentation or misinterpretation
over something never officially coaxed forth to begin with.

It was destroyed before it even posed a chance—
a chance to inspire, among the spires, in this Eternal Spiral
has been officially rendered exactly impossible.

Bombast's Avalanche

The re-exploded gutturals, resolute
and resonate, resounding
re-splendid and resplendent, splayed,
echoing through the centuries
like the voices of idolized idiots,
not void eschewing, but careening
off the walls of the Spirit,
and finding there the Truest of Echo-chambers.

Can inner-thought be just as profound and solid
as its corporeal cousin, the Diamond?

Building Gods

We are spilt onto this canvas for reasons
of which we do not know. That is,
if there even is a reason in the first place.
Our ancestors created creation by conjuring
Gods and inventing an interpretation of Existence
based on their limited knowledge of Nature coupled with Imagination.
These false focal points have led Humanity away
from the True Universal Realities that Existed
long before Mankind achieved its current state of Sentience
and ignored the already-Existing Existence into which they were born,
thus causing a flawed understanding of the Natural world which manifest
and carved itself into the bones and wombs of false manmade
societal Consciousness of the oncoming centuries.

The Omnipotence of *Is*

Is '*Is*' all it's really cracked up to be?
Why ask a person dressed as a torpedo such a question?
How would they know?
Split lip bandaged as you spilt milk
onto the sutures and statues of your skin.
The nose of the Sphinx.
The ears of the Grand Canyon.
The hair of the forest.
The eyes of the eyes.
Is doesn't need an explanation.
It just *Is*.
You are covered in cobwebs.
That's just the way it *Is*.

Rise and Refract

Spoken of   God raised
rosemary rosin bags
having arrived, arises,
reflecting up and down
among additional mist mixed with the Light
river straight wide lunar—
a bushel of push-all of Might
brings us commodious
run river
RISEN-rose   *rise! rise!*
irradiating a truckfull
of atomic Light → though mutated →
could still hold
Precious
Truth/
Newfangled
Sacrosanct
Answers.

The Hallucination of Nonexistence

Access to the axis of excess of thought.
You expressed disappointment at this
particular point in the appointment.
I noticed a hesitant resentment immanently
resonant like an aura's transcendent
remnant emanate over the interstate
into the Pool of Placation and beyond
into the Ethnosphere's massive congregation of Mankind's satiation
of the Suchness of this transmission's importance
as far as interpretation of the possibility
of a simultaneous deathful liveliness.

Timewise

The wisdom of clocks
is nothing more than a tedium
of perpetuation of expectant futurism.

A stich in time,
though no surgical equipment
can repeal this Monster Season;
this session which is not even a session
since it never existed and therefore can have no cessation
because time works in eternal kinks and tocks
and winks and knocks.

Combustible breastmilk is not
even enough to scare off
of the grandfather clock made of watches.
Time always gets its sickly sweet fix
of endless autonomy because
no matter what that ubiquitous omnivorous bastard
will always have its head
reared and ready to roar
in the here and now.

Digital Veins

Caliginous monstrosity clogation
of cognition   unhumbled robotic caligony
fills the air   beats upon the eardrums
        its metallic taste of wobbling noise

we endorphinlessly morph by the day
as we further depend on these mechanical monsters
to run amuck in our lives   and willingly allow it

so much so   these robotic beasts are infiltrating and
controlling
as they slowly tempt us with their bright screams of screens
of contagious connectivity   evolution spun metallic
soon to spring   and spoil the soil [soul]
as Mankind sticks its   perfectly uncut human
perceptions
heads and hands directly into the mouths of these vicious computer
screens
swimming with waning viscera in a pixilated pool
of pathetic predetermined angles of standpoints.

Wrinkled Thoughts

You reconcile the natural world in which you live
with ancient texts, therefore your perception
of the Universe is fundamentally flawed
because you are viewing everything
from a vantage point disconnected
from the precise scientific Truth
which has been proven by modern scientists.

Unlearn everything so you can be naïve enough to believe in everything
to the point where it has been so over-thought that these beliefs
become True.

To Live a Li(e)fe

So strutteral and rambunctational.
Meanwhile your swagger is so thickend outwhirled
that otherwise people have been snapshot-talking about
you behind your earlobes. I never did understandify why
you carry so much about the weight of what other flesheden
automatonians
thought about your emenatious animationness inny[buttonbelly]way.
Just ferment about them and leave your lifeing to yourself.
Youar' much bedder off this way. I don't care
about the idiocity they associalate with you.

Paradox

Paradox is just Paraguay pirouetting into pixelated post-mortem—
a perception to be experienced
in the minds of the living,
though does that not constitute Existence?—
do illusions ripe and real
as reality form an abstraction
of the extant world
no matter how spurious
they are known to be as far as the proportion
of their pithless pathetic plagiarism of life
they may pretend to predominate?

Do You Know How to Do This?

Do you know how to properly prop

the axle of the nexus in the supranova-
hole?

Do you know how to nozzle the fizzle
of the frisbee?

Do you know how to jargon a convex mind?

Do you know how to spread fresh honey across the quills of a
mutated razorback?

Do you know how to pulsate before the making of the making of
NOTHING?

Do you know how to hold a rock to your ear and hear its Existence?

Do you know of that mysterious entity our Consciousness
cannot understand and which creates Existence?

Simply Speaking

You are always glazing us with your thoughts.
How kind of you. Though, I'd rather you stop
your mutated mumblings rife with insanity
and instead speak Truth unto my ears.

It's my favorite song to hear the tonsils sprout.

People

People are people are made of people
like they're supposed to be made of
people with peopleskin and peopleheart
[can turn dark and black sometimes
like a lump of coal what with these
endless wars and mass genocides]
made purely of peoplequality [usually shoddy]
with their peoplelives and peopleperceptions
and peoplebrains communicating with the otherpeople.

The peoplesopoor are beyond lost on this personified planet.

Far Beyond the Predetermined Shackles

If none
of the mindless
crowds that populate
gas stations
and shopping malls
want anything
to do with you

then you're probably doing something Right.

No Body

I know I'm a   no body I know
no other bodys really care   about me
or maybe are just consumed with themselves

that's always been it!—
the consumption of every body by their own bodys
is the rigid stick of Imperialism ingrained in every body by Evolution

[some bodys have more than other bodys]
yet still be sure that this beast lies latent within even the lamest
limpest body
there is—   it is for this reason Imperialism will never die
it is the fire innate—   the fire thrown through the umbilical—
          as human [sometimes humane] bodys we'll just wait and
wait until eventually
we wipe away all of our bodys   and then I won't be the only no body
anymore
since every body will be a no body soon enough—

man's laughter   and   manslaughter

[human bodys are fashioning our nooses as we speak]

Construct of Nonexistence

Pleasantry
is actually
prevailing prisonheaded prevalence
Natalie is not a nucleus
brick bracken bitten bloody backwards burning bulldozers
inertia = UNDONE—
beginning from the beginning again—
finite—finalized when the falter phase fell fast
as nothing slow
reciprocal reconstructions reconvene
to revel in ambulatory prescript
oiled
with pith pocketed ideas purloined pounding outward
Proximity blossoms perennial Spiral
porously pulsed way beyond the past's previous penitentiaries of
pathetic pondering
pulverized by powerful portions of   pensiveness/ping!
of pig's eye   dead-on   damn straight
patterns perished proving purest
Freedom
Truth
Escape from simultaneous existence and nonexistence.

My Constant Mutation

I have not seen myself in years;
I am pale as a Russian bride;
a scented candle burns at my windowsill
but I smell nothing;
dust flitters through the air;
I am quiet as the dust;

I am becoming

something else.

Mock Burncolor

Thus begins a construct,
    begun within its physical
  encasement,
easing in,
not yet pulsating.
-

the paper reaches for the words
                or
the words reach for the paper
-

Autumnal breezes roared and
        the leaves began
    to turn
        a fiery hue—
this pulldown of Spirit
is cyclical
and has
become palpable
and predictable
and the usual
and something must be done about it
in order to switch
        from the dismal
                to the Uplift-able.

Sprout

A flower springs from
a puddle of blood on the floor

the scent of gunpowder
still adrift the air

the flower spilling
a slow sanguine ejaculate

crimson-droplets are equivalent to petals fallen off a rose

the seed of blood

purple then red as it
meets with the oxygen
outside the body

life taken,
life given
life sprung from death
just as it always has

just as this Earth Magnanimous has always done.

Remolded

The reflex
of the reverberation
reflected and refracted
down the rectangular roads
ravaging a reality recently revived
and repaired and repaved
counterbalanced concrete
in real time.
Reassured no one was relinquished from the realm
of reamed recognition.
Everyone regarded
the ravage of the repulsive ravines
now reigning and running randomly
throughout the rent ruins we pretend are not there.

Twig

Bent telephone poles adorn the crowded streets now cleared.
Holly and Jade cast out their midnight moans
to the confetti streets, the golden streets.

Bugs have come for us again.

Who are these people?

Ephemera

You stuck your hand out the window
just as the storm was fading away
saying you wanted to catch
the last drop of rain.

A Poem for Your Self

Encourage yourself in ways
no one has ever thought of

write secret hymns
that you find by accident
like poetic balloons of helium
to raise you up like a rooster
calling in the Day

write catastrophes yet to happen
and then stop them from happening

write the future you want for your Self
and then be the catalyst
which brings it to fruition

for all is connected—

a human mind can change sugar
into moss just by its positive thought output.

How I Bought the Universe

I sold my Tooth
for a Belly
and a Belly
for a Bean
and a Bean
for a Garden
and a Garden
for an Ability
and an Ability
for a Sustenance
and a Sustenance
for a Time
and a Time
for a Pondering
and a Pondering
for an Intellect
and the Intellect
slipped the Universe itself
right into the palm of my hand.

Falling Through Midnight

Stuck in an accurate
state of Pouring,
I finally notice the broken twigs and
this could be some type of Anti-Nirvana,
truthless and shallow as ever.

Fire cannot put out a fire
and, with luck, a random leaf
falls onto the ground which just happens
to be the special spot when it comes to Proximity
as it is miraculously unlicked by the flames.

At least no aftermath for now—

a cuckoo bird does not know it is a cuckoo bird.

There are uncontrollable
certainties in life
and this just happens to be one of them—
fortunately, the masses are distracted by gadgetry
and garments and endless arguments
and just carry on, unconcerned by the severity of it all.

Viperbite

who invented the game?—   the game invented itself
it's been run likewise longwise likethat
eversince—   human perception
has constructed itself and given birth
to the myriad Manmade realities
we buy into and eat of everyday
agreeing to agree that this is this
and that is that—   yass—
          mutual agreement of thoughtless people—
thisisthis and thatisthat

yass, that is the stuff Manmade realities are
constructed of.

Extant

Genuflection lost its mother to a Caesarian Section.
I quickly felt pangs of sorrow and showed
it some affection. Just enough to stifle
the mandatory saddened vexation
which haunts the mind without cessation.
The deliberate extension of an extinct Sentience
new to nonexistence is lulled out of obliviousness,
brought forth, and given implementation, due to
the frustration of circumstance which can arise
among such existential navigations.

A Letter to Mirrorism

Dear Mirrorism,

of the learned Manmade
rectangular world of monotony
sneezed into the brain
by infectious props of biased proclivity.
Commercial after commercial
billboard after billboard
teacher after insane teacher—

you best be
on the lookout!
I've been thinking
and have discovered
how to shake these shackles.
I've been swirling upon Spirals outward
into the Great Fathomlessness ever since.

Sincerely,

One of your *former* slaves.

Acknowledgements

"Lucky Number Never," "Rise and Refract," and "Digital Veins" were originally published in *Otoliths*.

"The Verge" was originally published in *Epigraph Magazine*.

"Bombast's Avalanche," "Simply Speaking," "Falling Through Midnight" were originally published in *The Wagon Magazine*.

"Building Gods" was originally published in Essential *Existentialism Anthology*.

"Timewise," "No Body," and "Ephemera" were originally published *in Harbinger Asylum*.

"To Live a Li(e)" was originally published in *The Curly Mind*.

"Paradox" was originally published in *Duane's PoeTree*.

"People" was originally published in *Unlikely Stories*.

"Far Beyond the Preconceived Shackles" was originally published in *Anti-Heroin Chic*.

"Construct of Nonexistence" was originally published in *X-Peri*.

"My Constant Mutation" was originally published in *Indiana Voice Journal*.

"Mock Burncolor" was originally published in *The Bhubaneswar Review*.

"Sprout" was originally published in *First Literary Review-East*.

"Remolded" was originally published in *PPP Ezine*.

"A Poem for Your Self" was originally published *in Fredericksburg Literary and Arts Review*.

"How I Bought the Universe" was originally published in *The Ibis Head Review*.

"Viperbite" was originally published in *SPAM Magazine*.

"A Letter to Mirrorism" was originally published in *Scarlet Leaf Review*.